A GREEK POTTER

Series Editor:
Giovanni Caselli

Illustrations:
Giuliano Fornari

Series Design:
Caselli Associates

Story Consultant:
Sean Hettesley

Book Editor:
Fiona Macdonald

Production:
Susan Mead

This edition published in 1992 by
Peter Bedrick Books
2112 Broadway
New York, NY 10023

Published by agreement with Simon & Schuster Young Books
Simon & Schuster Ltd, Hemel Hempstead, England

Library of Congress Cataloging-in-Publication Data
Caselli, Giovanni, 1939–
    A Greek potter.

    (Everyday life series)
    Summary: Observes a potter and his family living in
Athens in 420 B.C., a time of the Olympics, a great
festival to Athena, and the construction of many temples,
and describes the potter at work making and decorating
pots. Includes illustrations of tools and equipment he
and his family might have used in their daily lives.
    1. Pottery, Greek – Juvenile literature.   2. Vase-
painting, Greek – Juvenile literature.   [1. Pottery,
Greek.   2. Greece – Antiquities.   3. Greece –
Civilization – To 146 B.C.]   I. Fornari, Giuliano, ill.
II. Title.   III. Series: Everyday life series (New York,
N.Y.)
NK3840.C37   1986   738′.0938   85-30637

ISBN 0-87226-101-8

Printed and bound by
Henri Proost, Turnhout, Belgium
5 4 3 2

A
GREEK
POTTER

Giovanni Caselli

PETER BEDRICK BOOKS

NEW YORK

Contents

Introduction

The Greek family in this story lived in Athens during the last half of the fifth century BC. At that time, the city was rich and powerful, and a center for culture and the arts.

The story is set in 420 BC, an exciting year. The Olympic Games were held at midsummer, which was the Greek New Year. The games were so important that even the Peloponnesian War, which was going on between Athens and Sparta, was temporarily stopped. It was also a year for the Panathenaea, the great festival for the goddess Athena. The Athenian citizens held a festival for their goddess every year, but an especially splendid celebration took place every four years.

Pericles, the great Athenian leader, had died of the plague 10 years before in 430 BC, but work was still going on at all the magnificent temples he had ordered to be built. The most famous of these was the Parthenon, a temple to Athena on the Acropolis, a fortified hill in the centre of Athens. The building, and the great gold and ivory statue of Athena which stood in it, were the work of Pheidias, the most famous sculptor in Ancient Greece. The Athenians were very proud of their artists and craftsmen.

In this story, Meidias the potter and his family live in the Ceramicus, an area of Athens which lay between the city wall and the Agora, or market place. This was the potters' quarter.

The potters exported many of their pots to Italy, where they were used as grave decorations. Many of them survived until modern times, unlike Athenian household pottery which, naturally, got broken. That is why we know so much about Greek pottery and how it was made.

At the end of this book you can see some detailed pictures of the tools and equipment that Meidias the potter and his family might have used in their daily lives. There are also suggestions for books to read.

An Early Start

Apollodorus rubbed the sleep from his eyes and stifled a yawn. The sun had not yet risen but he and his father were already eating their breakfast.

'I don't suppose anyone else in Athens is even awake yet,' he grumbled.

'Eat up, son!' His father, Meidias, smiled at him encouragingly. 'We've a long journey ahead of us this morning.' He took a large gulp of the wine-and-water mixture which was the family's usual drink. Apollodorus dipped a piece of hard, coarse bread into his drink – it made it easier to chew – and crammed some more grapes into his mouth.

'Exactly where are we going, father?' he mumbled.

'Don't speak with your mouth full,' his mother, Daphne, scolded. 'You're going to Phalerum. It's by the sea. There's an old sea wall and some tumbledown houses.'

'It used to be the main port for Athens before Piraeus was built,' added his father. 'You may see some ships if you are lucky.'

Meidias was a potter. He made all the bowls, cups and plates the family used for eating and cooking. He also made special pots for the temples, beautifully-decorated dishes for rich people's houses and strong jars for merchants to pack their wine and oil in for export. He was well-known and respected in Athens. Today, he was going to Phalerum with some of his slaves to bring back fresh supplies of clay.

There was a stamping and jingling noise outside.

'Here are the slaves with the donkeys,' called Hermione, Apollodorus' sister, from the doorway. Meidias and Apollodorus got ready to leave.

'Don't forget to wear your hat, Apollodorus,' said his mother. 'It's not hot now, but it will be later on, and the sun will give you a headache if you don't cover up properly.'

Outside, the donkeys stood patiently, loaded with empty panniers for the clay, and with picks and shovels. Meidias nodded a greeting to his slaves. Then, as the sun was coming up over the horizon, they set off, across the sleeping city of Athens and along the road to Phalerum.

The Trip to Phalerum

Apollodorus plodded along beside the donkeys, the dust kicked up by their hooves stinging his eyes and throat. It was getting hot as the sun rose higher in the sky, and the crumbling wall that lined the edge of the road did not provide much shade. Suddenly he saw the glitter of sunlight on water.

'Look, look! The sea!' he shouted.

'Yes, we're nearly there now,' replied his father.

Apollodorus looked around with interest. On either side of the road stretched salty marshes, with mounds and hollows where clay had been dug. The donkeys came to a halt, and they climbed down.

'Hey, Apollodorus!' called his father. 'Come and help me choose some clay to take back with us! This is the best clay in the world, you know.' Meidias bent down to examine a large heap of crumbly clay.

'Why don't you dig up some fresh clay?' asked Apollodorus.

'Because clay is easier to work if it has been left out to weather for some time,' explained Meidias. 'This lot looks about ready to take home.' He stood up. 'Come, it's too hot here. Let's have a break and eat.'

After lunch, Meidias dozed for a while and then roused the slaves to work. Apollodorus was too interested in exploring to rest. In the distance, he could see some boys playing on the top of the sea wall.

'We're counting the ships as they sail past,' the oldest boy explained. 'I've seen six warships so far.'

Apollodorus clambered up the wall to join them. They had spotted eleven merchant ships and four more warships by the time he heard his father calling him. It was time for the long trek home.

Preparing the Clay

Next day there was a lot of work to be done. The new clay had to be prepared so that Meidias could use it to make pots. Apollodorus was meant to help with this, but he did not like doing it.

In the workshop, the slaves were already hard at work. The new, raw clay had to be broken up into small pieces and thrown into stone-lined troughs set into the workshop floor. Two of the slaves emptied jugs of water into the troughs, and mixed it with the clay until it all turned into a thick liquid. As they did this, the grit and sand in the raw clay sank to the bottom of the trough, leaving a layer of fine, semi-liquid clay above. The slaves then scooped this fine clay into another trough, and left it outside for the sun to evaporate the water from the mixture. Later on, the slaves would have to walk up and down in the trough, treading the clay with their feet until it became a stiff, sticky mass.

That afternoon, Meidias came in to the workshop. He looked around for his son.

'Where's Apollodorus? He should be helping you! That clay's still not ready to use. It needs wedging now.'

Apollodorus came running in. He had been playing with Ajax, his dog, in the courtyard. He sighed, but took up a handful of clay. He banged and rolled it on the tabletop until it was smooth and free of air bubbles. He knew this was necessary because air bubbles trapped in the clay would make the pots explode in the kiln, but he still found it very hard work, and boring, too. When he had finished, a slave rolled the clay into balls and wrapped them in damp cloth to stop them drying out.

Work over at last, Apollodorus was allowed to go out with his friend Talos to the Acropolis, the high cliff at the center of the city of Athens. There they saw lots of new building going on. They stopped in front of the great statue of the goddess Athena made by Pheidias, the sculptor.

'Isn't it amazing!' said Apollodorus, in awe.

'Yes,' replied Talos. 'Do you know that the spear tip is made of real gold? Sailors can see it for miles around and use it as a landmark.'

Meidias at Work

Although he did not like preparing the clay, Apollodorus loved to watch his father working with it.

'Sit and watch quietly,' said Meidias sternly. 'Don't interrupt me.' He turned to the slave who was helping him. 'I'm ready for the wheel now.' The slave began to turn the wheel. Meidias set a lump of clay securely in the middle of the wheel and, wetting his hands every so often in a bowl of water at his side, molded the lump into a rough round shape.

Apollodorus watched fascinated as his father pushed his thumbs into the spinning clay to make a bowl shape, then pulled up the walls of clay with his fingers, transforming the bowl into a tall pot.

'That's it! Apollodorus, pass me the wire.' Apollodorus handed his father a length of twisted wire. Meidias pulled it carefully between the bottom of the pot and the wheel to cut the pot free. He gave the pot to a senior slave who put in on the shelf to dry with others made that morning. In a few hours it would be hard enough to handle gently.

'Now pass me one of the pots I made earlier.' Meidias set the pot upside down on the still-turning wheel and skilfully trimmed off the spare clay with a special tool. One by one he tidied up all the pots he had made earlier on, until they were neat and even.

'Stop turning,' he said to the slave. 'That's all for this morning. Now, let's see what you can do, son!'

Apollodorus had his own wheel. He was quite a good potter and his father was proud of him, but today everything went wrong. The lump of clay flew off the wheel before he had even started to make a bowl shape.

'Oh no,' groaned Apollodorus. 'I'll never learn to do it. The clay either flies off or collapses into a messy heap. Why can't I just make figures? I like doing that.' Meidias shook his head.

'You must start again, Apollodorus. This is my trade and it will be yours too, when you grow up. I know it's hard work and you sometimes think you will never get it right, but you know the proverb: "To make pottery is to work hard".' And he handed his son another lump of clay.

Decorating the Pots

Meidias had some exciting news.

'You know that it will be the festival of Athena in July?' Apollodorus nodded. Athena was the patron goddess of the city of Athens. The Greeks also believed that she had invented the potter's wheel, so Meidias always said special prayers at her festivals.

'Well, I've been chosen to make some pots for the festival!' said Meidias. 'It's a great honor. The pots are to be prizes for some of the athletes. They must all have pictures of Athena on them. I can make beautifully-shaped pots, but I don't think I'm clever enough to draw pictures of our goddess. So I've asked Parrhasius and Agatharchus to come and help with the painting.'

Apollodorus knew that Parrhasius and Agatharchus were famous painters. He would enjoy watching them at work, but he had another reason to welcome them.

'When will they be coming?' he asked. 'I love to hear them talk about all the places they've seen. They've been everywhere!'

'Very soon,' replied Meidias. 'In a week or so. Now, come and help me get things ready for Parrhasius. You remember, he uses slip to decorate the pots instead of paint.'

Apollodorus did not mind helping to make slip, a thin, liquid clay. It was not hard work. He took care to make the mixture as smooth as possible, to make painting the pots easier. Meidias worked very hard to make the pots for Parrhasius and Agatharchus to decorate. Soon rows of beautiful pots stood ready on the shelf, still damp but firm. Apollodorus and the slaves polished them with lambswool to make a smooth surface for the decorating.

When both the artists arrived, they quickly got down to work. They outlined each figure with a sharp stick and brushed in the background with slip, using the mixture that Apollodorus had prepared. Apollodorus stood by to hand them the fine brushes they needed to paint the figures. When the pots were finished they were dried slowly to prevent them warping or cracking. They were, indeed, fit prizes for any champion at the Festival Games!

Firing the Kiln

As Apollodorus awoke, he remembered that something important was going to happen today. All the pots that Meidias had made over the past few weeks were to be baked in the kiln until they were hard and dry. At breakfast, Meidias looked rather thoughtful.

'What's the matter, father?' asked Apollodorus.

'I'm just thinking of all the things that could go wrong,' Meidias replied, frowning.

'What do you mean?' Apollodorus found it hard to believe anything dreadful could happen. He always enjoyed the excitement of building the fire in the kiln, with smoke and sparks flying from the flames.

'Well, if the pots are not thoroughly dry or if I've left any air bubbles in the clay, then they could explode. Or the fire could get too hot or not hot enough, or heat up too quickly, and then all my work will be ruined.' Meidias shrugged and then smiled. 'Perhaps I'm just being gloomy. Come on, let's start firing that kiln.'

Meidias and his senior slave stacked the pots carefully into the kiln, which was like a big oven built of clay. When it was full they sealed the door with clay.

Meidias lit the fire himself, but the slaves took over once it was burning steadily. Apollodorus helped them.

The fire was still burning fiercely long after sunset. Red smoke spangled with sparks flew up into the night sky. Meidias's family gathered around the kiln, eating honey cakes and drinking sweet wine. Suddenly there was a loud hammering at the courtyard door.

'Who can that be at this time of night?' said Daphne.

Two Athenian policemen came in.

'We saw the smoke and flames and thought we had better check that everything was in order.' The light from the fire flickered against their brightly-colored clothes. Athenian policemen were public slaves. They were brought from Scythia, a country to the north of Greece. They wore their own local costume as a kind of uniform.

'Everything is all right, thank you,' said Meidias. 'It's kiln-firing day, and going very well. But take a cup of wine before you go, for your trouble.'

Apollodorus tried to hide a yawn, but Daphne saw him. 'Off to bed, now, my lad!' she said. 'You've had enough excitement for one day.'

The Festival of Athena

It was the last day of the Panathenaea, the great festival of Athena. The celebrations had started with a torchlight race beginning outside the city walls and ending at the Acropolis. Apollodorus and Hermione had watched from the flat roof of their house. In the dark the runners were invisible and the torches they carried had darted through the darkness like fireflies. The winner of the race lit the fire on the altar of Athena to show that the festival had really begun.

During festival week there had also been music competitions, horse races, plays and athletic contests. Apollodorus had wished he could be in several places at once so he could see everything. All the special pots Meidias had made had been presented to the winners.

Apollodorus had even managed to sell some of his little statues as souvenirs. They seemed very popular with tourists from the other Greek states who had come to Athens for the festival.

Today there would be a great procession through the city. Meidias and his family had got up early to make sure of a good viewing place near the Acropolis.

'Look, here they come!' The crowd cheered as the procession marched slowly into view. It was led by girls carrying bowls of olive oil, in honor of the goddess. Apollodorus gasped as he caught sight of a magnificent ship. It seemed to be sailing on dry land! When it got closer, he could see that it was pulled by 100 white oxen. He had never seen so many beasts all together. The ship was brightly painted and something that looked like a huge banner with pictures on it hung from its mast.

'That's the Peplos,' explained Daphne. 'It's embroidered with scenes showing the goddess Athena's battle with the Giants. When the procession reaches the foot of the Acropolis, the people will carry the Peplos up the steep hill, and drape it over the great statue of Athena.'

'Then what happens? What happens to the ship, and to the oxen?' asked Apollodorus.

'Well, the oxen are sacrificed by the priests and their meat is roasted,' said Daphne. 'Then everyone shares in the feast. Come along! Are you feeling hungry?'

The Ship from Egypt

'Wake up! Father is going to Piraeus – he says you can go with him if you hurry.' Apollodorus was wide awake at once. He dressed quickly and snatched some breakfast. Soon, he and his father were on their way.

When they reached Piraeus, the port was bustling with life. Apollodorus stayed close beside his father.

'Where are we going?' he asked.

'To see Gorgias, the merchant,' explained Meidias, as they threaded their way through the crowd. 'He is a good customer of mine. He buys lots of big jars to export wine and olive oil. Now he wants me to make some more household pots and little figures to send to Italy. That's his warehouse, over by the quayside.'

'Hello, it's good to see you.' Gorgias led them into the warehouse and offered them wine and water. He and Meidias sat down to discuss orders.

'Do you feel brave enough to go down to the waterfront alone?' Gorgias said to Apollodorus. 'An Egyptian merchant ship has just come in. It might be interesting to watch.'

Apollodorus found the Egyptian galley at the quayside. Slaves and porters staggered down the gangplank carrying bales of rich and rare goods for the people of Athens to buy. There were bundles of brilliant silks, mysterious jars of spices and incense, and huge, curving tusks of ivory brought from the hot lands of Africa, far to the south. There were rare and beautiful animals, too; monkeys, apes, peacocks, and fierce cheetahs in strong wooden crates.

Suddenly the crowd parted and a string of dull-eyed men, chained together, stumbled through. They were captives, brought to Athens to be slaves. There were more slaves than free citizens in Athens. Skilled slaves, like Meidias's men were well-treated, but unskilled slaves had to carry out the dirty, dangerous work that no one else would do. Apollodorus had often heard his father say that slaves were only barbarians, and did not have the same feelings as civilized Greeks, but he could not help pitying the men in chains, all the same.

At the Market Place

Apollodorus loved going out to sell the pots that his father made. He always did well, and if he sold any of his own work he was allowed to keep the money. Best of all, it gave him the chance to go to the Agora, the market place of Athens.

The Agora was the center of the city's life. Merchants, traders, farmers and craftsmen of all kinds went there to buy and sell. After a couple of hours, Apollodorus decided to take a break from selling and wandered about, looking at the tempting displays of goods all around. Suddenly a group of young soldiers in full armor swaggered past.

'Only another eight years,' Apollodorus said to himself, 'and I'll be one of them.' When he was eighteen, Apollodorus would have to serve for two years in the army, ready to defend the city in time of war. Sometimes, he could hardly wait to leave home and the hard work of the pottery. He had heard many stories of brave battles fought by the Athenians against other Greek cities.

With a groan, he packed up his unsold pots and made his way home. Pottery was very heavy to carry! Sometimes, he and Meidias were summoned to a rich man's house. They had to take samples of their best pots with them. Apollodorus always grumbled as they went along. But Meidias's work was so good that they rarely left a customer's house without selling at least one item. That made the journey worthwhile.

Other customers called at the workshop to buy pots. It was one of Apollodorus's jobs to arrange a display of Meidias's pottery in the street outside their house. He was kept busy making sure that the display looked clean and tidy. Dust from the street soon covered everything if he wasn't careful.

A Visit to Grandfather

It was autumn. In spite of the sunshine, there was a sharpness in the air.

'It's nearly time for the olive harvest,' Daphne said to Meidias, as the family were eating their evening meal one night. 'Your father will be expecting us soon.' Apollodorus's grandfather had a farm outside Athens. Every year the family went to help him with the olive harvest. It was hard work, but the change from life in the city made it seem like a holiday.

'I hadn't forgotten,' Meidias replied. 'It will be good to work outside for a while.'

Two days later, the family set off, leaving the slaves in charge of the house and workshop. Daphne and Hermione travelled in a cart drawn by mules, and Meidias and Apollodorus rode on their donkeys.

Grandfather was waiting to welcome them.

'It's good to see you all again! By the gods, Apollodorus, how you've grown! You'll be able to knock the olives down without climbing the trees!'

The next day, Apollodorus, Meidias and Grandfather, with some slaves, began the harvest.

'Remember, Apollodorus,' Grandfather said, 'that you must treat the olive trees with respect. They are a gift from our goddess Athena. It's against the law to damage or uproot them.'

Carefully, Apollodorus and some of the farm boys climbed the trees and shook the olives down, while the men beat the branches with sticks. Then the olives were gathered up in baskets and taken to the olive press where the oil was squeezed out of them.

After a week of hard work, the olive harvest was finished. Grandfather organized a feast to celebrate. 'I've been fattening up one of the pigs for a special treat,' he said happily. No one ate much meat in Greece because all the fertile land was needed to grow wheat and there was little room left over for animals.

One day, shortly before they left for home, Grandfather took Apollodorus up to the beehives which he kept on the slopes of Mount Hymettus. Apollodorus got stung a couple of times.

'Don't worry, Grandfather,' he said. 'It's worth it for a pot of the best honey in Greece.'

New Year's Eve

Daphne was busy in the part of the house that was set aside for her, for her daughter Hermione, and their female slaves. There was always such a lot to do! The slaves helped with the heavy work, such as carrying fresh water from the communal well every day, or grinding the wheat for making bread, but Daphne liked to do most of the cooking herself. She also made clothes for all the family.

She was spinning fine wool now, which she planned to weave into cloth to make some new clothes for herself and also for Apollodorus. 'He's growing so quickly!' she said to Hermione.

Hermione could not really hear what her mother was saying, because she was washing her hair. One of the slaves was helping her. There was a lot of splashing and giggling from their corner of the room. Hermione had already finished her bath. She had sponged herself with water from a large basin, and then rubbed olive oil all over herself. When she scraped this off with a bronze scraper, called a strigil, all the dirt came off with it. Then she splashed herself with scented water before putting on clean clothes.

They were getting ready for the celebrations which would take place that evening.

26

It was New Year's Eve. Meidias had had a very good year and so there were to be prayers of thanksgiving in front of the family's altar to the goddess Athena.

Meidias and Apollodorus stopped work in the pottery earlier than usual, and went to the men's part of the house to wash and change into clean clothes.

When Meidias was ready, he called the household together. They all walked through the house to the courtyard, where there was a small altar to the goddess Athena, protector of the city of Athens and patron of potters. Meidias offered his prayers of thanksgiving.

'Great Athena, I thank you for the good fortune you have sent me this year. I pray that you will continue to smile on me and my household for the year to come.'

Picture Glossary

Ancient Greece was made up of a number of small city states, the largest of which was Athens. About a quarter of a million people lived in Athens, of whom three-quarters were slaves.

Athens was the center of the Greek world at the time of the story. The map (above) shows the most important regions. Some of them united under the leadership of Sparta to challenge the power of Athens in 431 BC.

Greek clothes were based on rectangles of linen or wool cloth. Men wore a himation (cloak) over their short tunics, or chitons (1). Women wore longer chitons in 431 BC.

Meidias the potter would have made many different kinds of pots, mostly decorated with red figures on a black background. For use in the home there were large storage jars (9), some with lids; three-handled water jars, or hydrias (10); various types of jugs (11); jars called kraters for mixing wine with water (12); and drinking cups (13). Sometimes the potter would decorate his work with pictures of himself at the wheel or of an artist painting (14). Potters also made little perfume bottles (15) and cosmetics jars (16).

Dorian chitons (2) were fixed at the shoulders with two clasps, like the gold brooch (5). Ionian chitons (6), were fixed all the way along the arms. Gold jewelry, like the earring (4), was popular, as were bronze mirrors (3). Clothes were stored in wooden chests (7). Greek shoes and sandals (8) were made of leather.

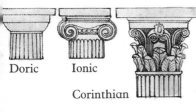

Doric   Ionic

Corinthian

The Greeks decorated the tops, or capitals, of their pillars in three ways (above).

6

Prosperous men such as Meidias lived in houses built of sun-dried bricks (above). The plan of the ground floor shows how the central courtyard was surrounded by reception and dining rooms, storage rooms, slave quarters and workshops. Upstairs were the bedrooms and women's apartments. The roof could be tiled or flat.

Theater-going was very popular. The open-air theater at Epidaurus shows the bowl-shaped amphitheater designed so that every word from the stage could be heard throughout the theater.

Finding Out More

Books to Read

The following books contain information about life in Ancient Greece, and about the beautiful pottery made by potters such as Meidias, who lived and worked there:

G. Caselli **The First Civilizations** (History of Everyday Things series) Peter Bedrick Books 1985

J. E. Jones **Ancient Greece** (History as Evidence series) Warwick Press 1983

M. Gibson **Gods, Men & Monsters from the Greek Myths** (The World Mythology series) Peter Bedrick Books 1991

You will need an adult to help you read the following books, but they contain a lot of fascinating information:

H. D. Kitto **The Greeks** Peter Smith Publishers 1988

R. Ling **The Greek World** (Making of the Past series) Peter Bedrick Books 1989

J. Pinsent **Greek Mythology** (Library of the World's Myths and Legends) Peter Bedrick Books 1982

PRINTED IN BELGIUM BY

proost
INTERNATIONAL BOOK PRODUCTION